The *Baroque Era*

The Life, Times, & Music Series

The *Baroque Era*
The Life, Times, & Music Series

Peter O. E. Bekker, Jr.

Friedman/Fairfax Publishers

A FRIEDMAN/FAIRFAX BOOK

ISBN 0-9627134-4-9

THE LIFE, TIMES, & MUSIC SERIES: THE BAROQUE ERA
was prepared and produced by
Friedman/Fairfax Publishers
15 West 26th Street
New York, New York 10010

Editor: Nathaniel Marunas
Art Director: Jeff Batzli
Photography Editor: Grace How
Production Director: Karen Matsu Greenberg

Designed by Zemsky Design

Grateful acknowledgement is given to authors, publishers, and photographers
for permission to reprint material. Every effort has been made to determine
copyright owners of photographs and illustrations. In the case of any omissions,
the Publishers will be pleased to make suitable acknowledgements in future
editions.

Printed in the United States of America

---—⊱♥︎—---

Acknowledgments

At Friedman/Fairfax Publishers: Michael Friedman, and
Mr. Roger Burrows for concocting this useful and unique series;
Karla Olson, a merciless negotiator but a writer's friend and inspiration;
and Nathaniel Marunas, whose keen eye for detail is informed by
impressive knowledge and insight. Many thanks to the staff at the
Lincon Center Branch of the New York Public Library for remarkable
dedication in what apparently are very difficult times.

---—⊱♥︎—---

Contents

Introduction

I t was an era of the sharpest contrasts and contradictions: a time of lib-

erating thought and oppressive politics; a time of humanism, which

celebrated the individual—and colonialism, which subjugated

millions; it was a time when empires rose and fell; a time

of rapid scientific discovery and also of the Inquisition;

and it was a time when the Church tried to counter the

Reformation that had split its ranks into Protestant and Catholic.

The Baroque was the final doorway of history that opened from

medieval times onto the Age of Enlightenment.

Right: This ornate Baroque era sculpture, Angel, is modeled after a drawing by Bernini and sits on Rome's Ponte del Angeli. Opposite page top: King Ferdinand's representatives are thrown from a window of Prague's Hradcany Palace.

Politics and Intrigue: An Era Shaped by War

The map of Europe changed dramatically during the century and a half that is now called the Baroque era, beginning with the Thirty Years' War, which blossomed in 1618 and quickly escalated into the first conflict to involve all of Europe. The Baroque came of age on that stage of political and religious aggression, and played itself out in the aftermath—literally in an entirely different world.

Sparked by a minor revolt at the Hradcany Palace in Prague—where two representatives of the Catholic King Ferdinand, a Habsburg, were thrown out of a window by Protestant noblemen—the Thirty Years' War ultimately led to a redrawn map of Europe and a considerable shift in its centers of power.

The Protestants were afraid of annihilation or at the very least, frightened that their influence would be blunted by Ferdinand's unrelenting campaign to assert his Catholic policies far and wide. It is likely that the nobles were justified in their fears. Ferdinand was a Catholic who not much later would be elected Holy Roman Emperor and dubbed Ferdinand II. He supported the Church's Counter Reformation, though his motives were much more earthly than divinely inspired: Ferdinand wanted to reassert the Holy Roman Empire as the primary political entity in central Europe and Italy; his main goal was to grab for himself and his Habsburg dynasty as much power in Europe as he could.

The Holy Roman Empire (962-1806)

The empire, comprising central Europe and Italy, had been around for more than six and a half centuries before the outbreak of the Thirty Years' War (1618-1648), but its influence waxed and waned depending on the inclinations and strengths of its emperors and popes. At the turn of the seventeenth century the most influential rulers were the local noblemen and regional princes who governed the principalities and city-states.

The theory of the empire was twofold: to encompass a society of Christians under the One Holy Catholic Church; and to be organized very much like today's corporations, under a hierarchical system, with an emperor serving as chairman of the board. The emperor was to be the protector and defender of faith and the papacy. But the empire was too large for any one sovereign to govern effectively. In addition, there were problems at the top because popes and emperors sometimes tried to dominate each other. The ambitions of men and nations often led to divisive intrigues and rebellions.

The empire was born in 962 when Germany's King Otto I was crowned "emperor of the Romans" by Pope John XII in gratitude for Otto's help in protecting the Papal States from the ambitious king of Italy. From that time forward, German kings claimed the right to be emperor, and most of them declared themselves as such or were crowned by the pope.

The Thirty Years' War, launched as a religious crusade by Ferdinand II (who died before the war ended), permanently crippled the Holy Roman Empire. His successor, Ferdinand III, was left with little more than a title by the time the Treaty of Westphalia, among others, ended the conflict.

Napoleon I drove in the final stake with his successful campaigns against Austria and its allies in 1797 and 1801. By 1806, annexations and secessions had prompted emperor Francis II to abdicate and declare the Holy Roman Empire dissolved.

Above: Map of the Holy Roman Empire.

The opponents in this conflict were guided by religious imperatives and, as a result, their battles turned into holy wars. With so much at stake, each side easily found allies. This expanded the conflict, sometimes geometrically, because the allies, mostly neighboring states, were already involved in their own religious and political entanglements.

Charles II returned to the throne upon the collapse of Cromwell's Commonwealth and Protectorate.

Ferdinand enlisted his cousins for help: King Philip III of Spain and Duke Maximilian of Bavaria. He was joined also by Poland, though Poland would later switch sides in an alliance with Sweden.

Old tensions between the Spanish and the Dutch flared up early in the war. That rivalry was played out not only in Europe but also around the globe—in Africa, South America, and the Caribbean—where both nations had colonies. Spain was kept especially busy when, in 1640, Portugal again decided to assert its independence and battled its larger neighbor for desirable territories abroad.

France was on the sidelines for the first half of the war. King Louis XIII, a Catholic, was the Habsburgs' main rival in Europe. As time passed, Louis became increasingly alarmed about Ferdinand's victories. He finally decided that a preemptive strike was the best way to help subdue his competitor. He declared war on Spain in 1635 and entered the fray on the Protestant side in an alliance with Sweden, the Netherlands, and a group of Protestant German princes.

France's entry into the Thirty Years' War eventually brought the conflict to a stalemate. So many alliances had been formed that it became impossible to shift the balance of power in favor of any state or group of states. The only way for the combatants to stand down from their military postures was to seek peace. It was a process that took quite a long time since all the sides were negotiating from a position of some strength. Each of the players tried to win as much from the peace settlements as they had tried to gain from their military adventures.

Mural depicting Baroque era pomp in Saxony (Germany).

The Treaty of Westphalia took five years to conclude even after the main combatants had put down their swords. The Habsburgs emerged with far less influence in Europe than they had had at the outset. France emerged as the dominant nation in Western Europe; Sweden was eminent in the Baltic; and the German princes were set free to govern their domains as they wished with no interference from the emperor. Because Ferdinand and the Habsburgs failed in their mission to consolidate power, the Church also suffered. The Thirty Years' War turned out to be the last war of religion in Europe. Regional rulers were thereafter able to choose for their subjects whatever religion they desired. Religion, and the papacy, would no longer play significant roles in determining national allegiances.

The War of Spanish Succession was waged against France's "Sun King," Louis XIV, who had upset the balance of power in Europe by accepting for his grandson the inheritance of Spain's Charles II, who died childless. By accepting the inheritance, Louis broke an agreement with the British that he would split Charles' territories with the Austrian Habsburgs.

France and its Spanish and Bavarian allies faced a grand alliance of Britain, the German princes, the Austrian Habsburgs, the United Dutch Provinces, Portugal, and Savoy in what was a long and bloody war. Begun in 1701, the fighting continued until 1714, when political developments broke a military impasse. The Peace of Utrecht awarded Spain and its colonies to Philip V, a Bourbon king, but kept France separate. The Dutch won British assurances of protection against French aggression. Austria was awarded the Spanish Netherlands, Sardinia, Milan, and Naples. Britain emerged as the world's leading colonial and commercial power, mostly on the strength of its Navy.

The Reformation

A backlash against corruption in the Church, the Reformation began in 1517 when Martin Luther, a university professor in Wittenberg, Germany, posted an invitation to debate the Church practice of selling indulgences.

The Church was riddled with excesses and abuses throughout medieval times and into the Renaissance. Pope Innocent III recognized even in 1215 that reform was necessary. The ordinary man suffered in general from domination by the Church, and specifically because of rivalries within the church and political deals or conflicts between royals and the clergy. There was nepotism, financial extravagance, and—probably the most cynical practice of all—the selling of indulgences. This was a way for those who could afford it to be "cleansed" of sin, but it was recognized as a dangerous barrier to sincere repentance and spiritual healing.

With the advent of the Renaissance, thought and study were stressed and the level of education rose in most of Europe. Gutenberg introduced moveable type, which allowed a more rapid spread of ideas, including those of the Protestants (who had had enough of Church abuses).

Luther was excommunicated as a heretic, but his ideas for a reformed religion nevertheless caught on. Lutheranism became the recognized religion for Sweden, Norway, Finland, and Denmark, and spread quickly throughout the rest of Europe, eventually giving rise to Calvinism and other reform doctrines.

Martin Luther sows the seeds of Protestantism.

The Counter Reformation

Alarmed by the quick acceptance of Lutheranism and other Protestant doctrines, the Catholic Church launched an internal movement in the 1500s to address its own failings and stifle what it saw as a mutiny by its adherents.

There were many repressive elements to the Counter Reformation, in addition to a few significant attempts to heal the serious rifts through genuine spiritual and ecclesiastical reform.

The prime example of the repressive side was the Inquisition, which had been a fixture of life throughout Europe

Pope Paul III

from the thirteenth century. In 1231, following the lead of Holy Roman Emperor Frederick II, Pope Gregory IX promulgated rules that permitted civil authorities to seize and burn convicted "heretics." This led to a more or less organized judicial circuit of Inquisitors who traveled about, hearing cases against those who were suspected of defying orthodox religious teachings. Many of the defendants were simply political irritants to the local establishment, which trumped up charges against them. Other defendants were members of sects whose spiritual practices did not align with Catholic theology. Still others were suspected of being alchemists,

witches, sorcerers, or sexual aberrants. It was not uncommon for "confessions" to be forced from defendants by sessions on the "rack," which painfully stretched a persons's limbs, or by torture with burning coals.

But Paul III, who became pope in 1534, also convened the Council of Trent to study, debate, and answer the fundamental doctrinal questions raised by the Protestant reformers. He sanctioned new, more active religious orders such as the Jesuits, who brought a zealous reinterpretation of strict Catholic dogma into religious schools, to charity works, and also to the newly discovered provinces abroad, including both North and South America.

Still, Paul III and his immediate successors did not meaningfully address the repressive character of the Inquisition, which by the end of the sixteenth century had spread throughout the colonized world as the Spanish Inquisition. The latter was an especially brutal undertaking that persecuted thousands of converted natives in the Spanish and Portuguese colonies in the Americas. The Inquisition was not ended in Spain and Portugal until the early 1800s.

Another repressive aspect of the Inquisition, The Index of Forbidden Books, was not abolished by the papacy until 1965. The Index, begun in the fifth century, was a list of teachings, manuscripts, and books that were banned as antithetical to Church dogma.

Heretics were often burned at the stake during the Inquisition.

Oliver Cromwell (1599-1658), Puritan English statesman.

The English Civil War pitted royalists against parliamentarians. It was comprised of three wars involving two kings of England and those who sympathized with the growing and increasingly prosperous middle class (most notably Oliver Cromwell, who ruled England following the execution of Charles I).

By 1642, the gentry and merchants had become dissatisfied with their lack of representation in policy and lawmaking. The stubborn King Charles I refused to bend to democratic ideas and paid little attention to the increasingly hostile voices in the House of Commons. Nevertheless, Charles, who did not have much inherited wealth, often insisted that Parliament raise taxes and provide funding for his numerous foreign campaigns.

As passions mounted, both sides raised armies. The king's Cavaliers swept to early victories against the Parliamentary forces, known as Roundheads, but the tide eventually turned. Charles surrendered and was held prisoner, but managed to escape. He concluded a treaty with the Scots, who then invaded England. But Oliver Cromwell beat back the assault and Charles was eventually caught and executed.

His son, Charles II, resumed the fight but was no match for Cromwell's armies, who crushed his allies in Ireland and Scotland. Charles II was forced into exile, returning in 1660 when Cromwell's Commonwealth and Protectorate collapsed. The king's return to England was known as the Restoration and it was conditioned on an amnesty for most of his enemies in England, and on his promise of religious toleration, a promise he promptly broke by cracking down on dissenters from the Church of England.

Fine Arts

Ideology and religion remained power-
ful forces in shaping the fine arts
during the Baroque era. Even though
its influence was on the decline, the
Church remained an imposing institution, particularly in such traditionally
Catholic societies as Italy, Spain,
Portugal, and central Europe. Born in
Italy, and seen most purely and vividly
in areas of heavy Church influence,

*The lute was an extremely popular instru-
ment at the dawn of the Baroque era.*

the Baroque style ultimately spread throughout the Western world, where
it was sifted and molded by regional influences.

    The Church required dynamic, vibrant imagery to illuminate the
spiritual core of its Counter Reformation and to serve as an ingredient in
its burgeoning missionary work. Royals and other wealthy influentials
wanted homes, palaces, and monuments that were opulent, distinctive,
and appropriate to their stations. It is just that kind of dynamic, dramatic,
grand style that charac-
terizes Baroque art, which
first emerged in the work
of two young artists: the
Flemish painter Peter
Paul Rubens, and the
Italian sculptor, painter,
and architect Giovanni
Lorenzo Bernini.

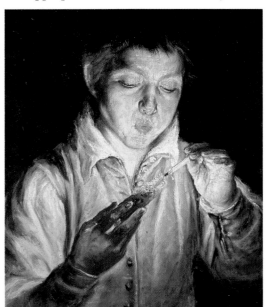

Opposite page: The Last Supper
by Peter Paul Rubens.
*Left: An example of El Greco's
dramatic use of light:* Boy
Blowing Over Hot Coals.

Bold and colorful, The Battle of the Amazons by Peter Paul Rubens shows the influence of the Renaissance master Titian on his work.

Peter Paul Rubens (1577-1640)

By any measure, Rubens was a Renaissance man. He lived and worked during the transition from the Renaissance to the Baroque and is credited, more than anyone else, with having transformed painting into the style that came to be called Baroque. A phenomenally productive artist, he was also a diplomat, a courtier, a teacher, and a man who involved himself in public affairs. He distilled the realistic tradition of Flemish art with the classical and imaginative innovations of Italian Renaissance painting to produce a striking new form that directly influenced the direction of painting and drawing in Italy, Spain, the Netherlands, and even England.

Rubens was already a master in the Netherlands when he arrived in Venice, at the age of twenty-one, to complete his artistic education. As court painter to the duke of Mantua, Rubens was impressed by the bold, colorful paintings of Titian, who inspired many of Rubens' later works. He naturally benefited from the influence of other Italian Renaissance masters and made contributions of his own in Rome and Spain, and, upon his return to Antwerp, also to northern Europe, where he reigned as the leading figure in art in the Spanish Netherlands.

A devout Catholic, Rubens used religious themes in his paintings. Unlike the dogmatic work of his less inspired contemporaries, however, Rubens' dramatic use of light and color brought a distinctive energy to his canvases. His fondness for bold forms reached its zenith in the 1620s when he completed, among other works, a twenty-one-painting theme for the Luxembourg Palace chronicling the life of Marie de Medici. Rubens operated a large studio dur-

Self Portrait, *Rubens*.

Rubens' Portrait of the Servant of the Young Isabella *depicts the future queen of Spain.*

ing this period in which skilled artists did most of the actual painting, working from sketches that Rubens made. This was an arrangement similar to the famous painters' workshops in Italy and it turned out thousands of canvases.

As a diplomat, Rubens helped conclude peace treaties between England and Spain, and also between the Spanish Netherlands and the Dutch. His patrons, Archduke Ferdinand and Archduchess Isabella, also gave him other, less visible diplomatic assignments. His ability was impressive enough to earn him a knighthood from Charles I of England, who also commissioned a ceiling painting called *The Allegory of War and Peace* for the Whitehall Palace in London.

Late in his life, Rubens abandoned religious paintings and turned out mostly landscapes and portraits.

El Greco (1541-1614)

Influential artists who lived and worked during the Baroque Era and whose names are remembered today include the Italians Michelangelo da Caravaggio who, along with Annibale Carracci, pioneered a revival of Greek, Roman, and Classical styles that had a great influence on the eventual development of the Baroque motif. In addition, Baroque painters began experimenting with a dynamic use of light, especially in the service of creating incredible spatial depth.

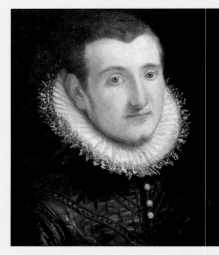

El Greco, born on Crete—at the time a dependency of Venice—was a painter who worked briefly in Italy and mostly in Spain. Noted especially for his later paintings, which featured abstract elements such as elongated figures and dramatic, flickering light, El

Self Portrait, *El Greco.*

Greco produced work of tremendous psychological power and intense, visionary, and even mythological impact.

Above: El Greco's *Portrait of* Giulio Clovio *contains characteristic elements of pathos and mystery, accented by a dynamic contrast of light and dark. Opposite page:* The Trinity, El Greco.

Rembrandt's largest painting, Night Watch, illustrates the painter's genius at infusing his canvases with drama and movement.

Rembrandt van Rijn (1606-1669)

Rembrandt, the Dutch artist, is remembered for his skillful paintings, drawings, and etchings, many of them of individuals or groups of people. He often experimented with different expressions for his subjects, and with contrasts of light and shadow designed to change the overall drama and effect of the composition. Rembrandt's brushwork is particularly admired for its emotional and textural range, and for its great subtlety of expression.

Above: Self Portrait *(age 34), Rembrandt. Below: A remarkable sensitivity to human expression is an important element in Rembrandt's work, as in* Lady and Gentleman in Black.

Sir Anthony van Dyck (1599-1641)

Van Dyck opened his own studio in Antwerp at age sixteen; by the time he was eighteen years old, the Flemish painter was a master of Antwerp's artist's guild. To develop an internationally recognizable style, van Dyck spent several years in Italy studying the work of Renaissance masters such as Titian. A colleague of Peter Paul Rubens, van Dyck is now considered second only to his famous countryman as the greatest European painter of the time. His work included mostly portraits and religious paintings.

Top: Van Dyck painted many portraits, religious canvases, and mythological scenes. Venus asks Vulcan to make Weapons for Aenas hangs in the Louvre. Above: Self Portrait, van Dyck.

Giovanni Lorenzo Bernini (1598-1680)

Another figure whose contributions helped define Baroque art, Bernini worked not only in paints, but also as a sculptor and an architect. Bernini is remembered for developing a detailed, realistic form of sculpture, and he was also responsible for the design of grand homes, elaborate churches, and some of the more spectacular architectural elements of St. Peter's Basilica in Rome.

The son of a painter, Bernini was born in Naples and, except for one trip to Paris at the invitation of King Louis XIV, he lived and worked his entire life in Rome. (On the Paris trip, in 1665, Bernini submitted designs for the Louvre, but his plans were not used.)

His works for the Basilica constitute a significant portion of his architectural legacy, and include the massive bronze canopy over St. Peter's tomb; the Altar of the Chair (Cathedra Petri), which enshrines the Chair of St. Peter and serves as the church's focal point; the intricate tombs of two popes (Urban VIII and Alexander VII); and a design for the oval piazza out front.

Two of the several churches he designed in Rome are Santa Bibiana and the oval church Saint Andrea al Quirinale. The Palazzo Chigi-Odescalchi is one of the outstanding examples of his secular architecture.

Of Bernini's surviving sculptures, three in Rome's Villa Borghese are widely acknowledged as masterpieces: *Rape of Proserpine* (1621), *Apollo and Daphne* (1622),

Opposite page: The bronze canopy designed by Bernini towers above St. Peter's tomb in the Basilica, Vatican City.
Above:Self Portrait, Bernini.

Bernini's oval church, Saint Andrea al Quirinale, in Rome.

Self Portrait, *Bernini*.

Daphne (1622), and *David* (1623). An extravagant "multimedia" work, *Ecstasy of St. Theresa*, encompasses sculpture, architecture, and painting. It was commissioned for the Cornaro Chapel of Rome's Church of Santa Maria della Vittoria.

Creations of the prominence and on the scale of those executed by Rubens and Bernini had a vast influence on the work of other artists. Even in France, where the cult of reason dictated classical restraint, a "classical-baroque" style emerged, with the magnificent Versailles Palace as its centerpiece. Baroque architecture was taken abroad to the Spanish and Portuguese colonies in the Americas, and in Protestant England, Sir Christopher Wren included Baroque aspects in his design for St. Paul's Cathedral.

Ecstasy of St. Theresa *(1645-1652)*.

Galileo lectures on his revolutionary view of the nature of the heavens.

Science & Philosophy

Philosophical thought and scientific theory historically have been the cause of endless discussion, debate, and controversy. This was particularly so during the Baroque, a time of such rapid scientific development that many long-held beliefs about the very foundations of the universe were called into question, and discovered to be factually unsound.

Nicolaus Copernicus (1473-1543)

Of the many mathematicians and scientists at work in Europe during the period, Galileo, Kepler, and Newton are remembered for fundamentally changing the way we think about our world. Each of them built upon the contributions of the others, but it was Nicolaus Copernicus, a Polish thinker, who provided the foundation for their subsequent discoveries when in 1543 he circulated a manuscript, "On the Revolutions of the Heavenly Spheres." In it, Copernicus questioned the long-held belief that the Sun and the other planets revolved around a stationary Earth; he suggested that the observable changes in the sky and the other celestial phenomena cited by Aristotle and Ptolemy to support that claim could be explained far more easily by a rotating Earth that revolved with other planets around a stationary Sun.

Galileo Galilei (1564-1642)

Galileo is credited with pioneering modern physics, mostly through his studies of motion. In his capacity as astronomer, he made important contributions to astronomy and telescopy. He built a number of advanced telescopes, came up with an explanation for the motion of tides, and determined that projectiles don't travel in straight lines, but rather in curved trajectories. Galileo taught mathematics at universities in Pisa and Padua. He challenged Aristotle's theories about falling bodies and the nature of the heavens by demonstrating mathematically that all objects fall at the same rate, regardless of their weight. His participation in a debate with philosophers over the significance of a supernova explosion in 1604 challenged the Aristotelian idea that change could not occur in the heavens. Galileo's *Dialogue*, published in 1632, was an impartial examination of the theories of both Copernicus and the second-century astronomer Ptolemy about the nature of the planets and their orbits. Its publication so angered the Church that Galileo was sentenced by the Inquisition to life in prison for suspicion of heresy. He was able to continue his studies when his sentence was commuted to house arrest, and published *Discourses and Mathematical Demonstrations*, the basis for a new kind of physics, in 1638.

Frontispiece of Galileo's Systema Cosmicum published in 1641.

Above: Sir Isaac Newton's study of light led him to conclude that white light is actually made up of many rays of different colors. Below: Geometric compass of the sort used by Galileo.

Copernicus' position was considered not only radical, but heretical. In fact, ninety years later Galileo was called to Rome during the Inquisition and sentenced to life imprisonment for disregarding an order never to teach Copernicanism. The sentence was later commuted to house arrest, but Galileo's work was banned in Italy.

The superstitions of the Church notwithstanding, Johannes Kepler used Copernicus' theory to formulate his view that the planets have elliptical, not circular orbits. Galileo Galilei proposed theories of motion that later helped Sir Isaac Newton come up with his Universal Theory of Gravitation and to pen what many consider the most profound scientific book ever published, *Philosophiae Naturalis Principia Mathematica* (Mathematical Principles of Natural Philosophy).

If Newton is remembered as the one who in his *Principia* collated the most advanced thinking of the day into a coherent scientific theory, Galileo is remembered as the thinker who urged that traditions and established thought must always be challenged by observable and measurable inquiry if science is to progress.

With science fragmented and still unaware of many basic truths, scientists of the Baroque era were often also considered philosophers. Likewise, since scientific inspirations frequently originated as philosophical thought, philosophers of the age frequently dabbled in science. Among the prominent philosopher-scientists of the time were René Descartes, Blaise Pascal, and the British political theorist John Locke.

Johannes Kepler (1571-1630)

Kepler was a strong supporter of Copernicus, who proposed nearly thirty years before Kepler was born that the Earth is not the center of the universe. While Copernicus theorized that the Earth and the other planets revolve around a stationary Sun, he also believed that their orbits were circular. Kepler proved mathematically that the orbit of Mars is in fact elliptical. That was one of the three Laws of Planetary Motion for which Kepler is now famous. He also made the connection between the speed at which planets travel in their orbits and their distances from the Sun, the foundation for Isaac Newton's later postulation of the Universal Theory of Gravitation. In 1627 Kepler published the *Rudolphine Tables*, a reference book detail-ing the orbits of the planets. Kepler may also have been the first science fiction writer; he wrote about a trip to the Moon, and even speculated about the possibility of life there.

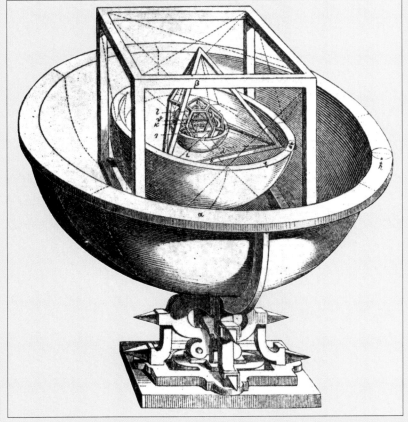

A device used by Kepler to illustrate his early theory of planetary orbits.

Franz Hals' portrait of René Descartes *hangs in the Louvre.*

René Descartes (1596-1650)

Despite a traditional Jesuit education, Descartes decided as a young man to concoct a unified science of nature. His major goals were to devise an absolutely reliable method of reaching Truth and to provide a conceptual foundation for the new physics of Copernicus and Galileo. Descartes believed that mathematics was the only absolute method of establishing reality and he came up with a system of withholding his belief in anything that was not absolutely unquestionable. In his work as a mathematician, he unified algebra and geometry and developed what would come to be called Cartesian coordinates; as a philosopher, Descartes explored the idea of "universal doubt," concluding that the only thing that could not be doubted was thinking itself. He summed this up in his famous statement, "I think, therefore I am."

Sir Isaac Newton (1642-1727)

Probl I

Investiganda est curva Linea ADB in qua grave a dato quovis puncto A ad datum quidvis punctum B vi gravitatis suæ citissime descendet.

Solutio.

A dato puncto A ducatur recta infinita APCZ horizonti parallela et super eadem recta describatur tum Cyclois quæcunque AQP recta AB (recta et si opus est producta) occurrens in puncto Q, tum Cyclois alia ADC cujus basis et altitudo sit ad prioris basem et altitudinem respective ut AB ad AQ. Et hæc Cyclois novissima transibit per punctum B et erit Curva illa linea in qua grave a puncto A ad punctum B vi gravitatis suæ citissime perveniet. Q.E.I.

SOLUTION OF THE PROBLEM OF THE BRACHYSTOCHRONE, OR CURVE OF QUICKEST DESCENT, BY NEWTON.

Newton's solution to the problem of the "curve of quickest descent."

Arguably the world's greatest scientific thinker and natural philosopher, Newton, among his many accomplishments and contributions, laid the groundwork for the new mathematics of integral and differential calculus. Most of his "new math" was technically unprovable at the time because the mathematical resources necessary to double-check the accuracy of the results hadn't been invented yet. Still, Newton's techniques seemed to work just fine in practice, serving mostly as problem solving tools for computing areas, tangents, and the lengths of curved lines.

In optics and astronomy, Newton debunked the established notion that white light is a pure, uniform entity. He demonstrated that white light is actually comprised of a "bundle" of different colored rays (the spectrum) and that each type of ray is refracted in a slightly different way. Newton devised and built the first reflecting telescope, the result of his other explorations of light and optics.

Newton's Laws of Motion, Universal Theory of Gravitation, and *Principia* brought answers, or at least plausible explanations, to many of the loose ends and imponderable questions of existing physics and astronomy. His insights into mathematics and celestial mechanics advanced the development of those disciplines by at least several generations. In recognition of his work, Queen Anne awarded him a knighthood in 1708, the first such honor for a scientist.

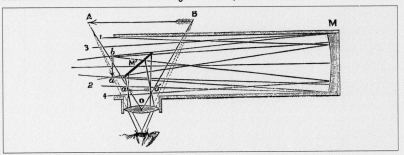

Newton designed and built the first reflecting telescope, a forerunner of today's largest and most efficient optical telescopes.

Blaise Pascal (1623-1662)

Pascal, a Frenchman like Descartes, influenced later generations of theologians and philosophers. His meditations on human suffering and man's faith in God, *Pensées* (Thoughts), preceded his own painful death from a stomach tumor at the age of thirty-nine. In "Pascal's Wager," his most famous theorem, he concluded that belief in God is rational because nothing will be lost by this belief if God does not exist, but if He does, one would lose everything by not believing.

Pascal's immediate contributions included a computing machine that is considered a predecessor of today's modern computers. (Pascal, the computer language used universally today, was named for the Frenchman.) He invented the syringe, and he also developed a Law of Hydrostatics, the practical application of which can be seen in the hydraulic press and air and hydraulic brakes.

John Locke (1632-1704)

The English philosopher and political theorist John Locke was an eminent gentleman and a friend to quite a few prominent seventeenth-century notables. In philosophy he is credited with founding British Empiricism, an outlook that equates knowledge with experience and identifies experience as the font of all ideas. Unlike the Rationalists, who held that the human mind is endowed with a certain number of innate, or "built-in," ideas, the Empiricists argued that everything one learns or knows must first be gathered through experience. In his *Essay Concerning Human Understanding*, Locke spoke of knowledge in terms of Newtonian Science, and he was another philosopher to believe that mathematics was the only irrefutable method of determining anything with certainty.

As a political theorist, Locke wrote extensively in favor of Liberalism. He disagreed with Thomas Hobbes' view of the world as a dangerous place in which citizens must surrender their individual rights to a supreme ruler in exchange for protection. In *Two Treatises of Government*, Locke argued that the purpose of a state is to protect the rights and liberties of its citizens; failing that, citizens have the right, and maybe even the duty, to rebel. In "A Letter Concerning Toleration," Locke defended freedom of religion, but not unequivocally.

Literature

The great writers of the Baroque era often wrestled with the classical theme of man's role in the scheme of things. Criticism and satire were popular forms, particularly in an age when radical new discoveries regularly upset the status quo. Poetry was also an ubiquitous form, and the most respected poet of the day was probably the Englishman John Milton.

John Milton (1608-1674)

An outspoken and scholarly man, Milton is best remembered for his epic poems *Paradise Lost* and *Paradise Regained*. During his lifetime he also raised his voice in protest against the monarchy, religious intolerance, and what he saw as the weaknesses and failings of the church and the clergy. When his second wife left him, Milton wrote *The Doctrine and Discipline of Divorce*, one of a number of pamphlets in which he argued in favor of divorce.

Milton was on the side of the Parliamentarians during the English Civil War and wrote passionately in favor of freedom of the press and against the restoration of the monarchy. He believed that monarchs

Blindness forced John Milton to dictate much of his work to his daughters.

can rule only with the consent of their subjects. That idea and Milton's views on religious toleration were not shared by Charles II. Milton was jailed briefly following the Restoration (possibly because of his writings), for the stated reason of having served as Secretary to Oliver Cromwell's Council of State. He was ultimately released after paying a fine.

John Dryden (1631-1700)

John Dryden was a contemporary of Milton and considered himself to be a spokesman for the sensibilities of his generation. Known mostly for his poetry, Dryden also wrote in many other forms: literary criticism, satire, comedy, and heroic tragedy.

Although he was definitely a man of shifting religious and political convictions, Dryden nevertheless wrote eloquently for and about whatever position he took. His *Heroic Stanzas*, for example, eulogizes Oliver Cromwell while his *Astraea Redux* celebrates the restoration of Charles II (following the collapse of Cromwell's Commonwealth and Protectorate). Furthermore, *Absalom and Achitophel* is a satirical attack on the English Puritans, the Whig Party, and the first Earl of Shaftsbury for conspiring to deprive the throne of England of its legitimate heir.

Dryden was England's Poet Laureate for a time. Of his poetry and his contribution to England's poetic tradition Samuel Johnson observed, "He found it in brick, and he left it in marble."

Right: An elaborate theater production at Versailles.

Jean-Baptiste Molière (1622-1673)
Like Shakespeare, Molière was not only a playwright but also an entrepreneur, founding theatrical companies in which he also acted and directed. Molière was known chiefly as the author of satirical comedies that reveal man's foibles and pretensions, and many of his plays are frequently performed today, a testament to the timelessness of his themes and the potency of his art. *Tartuffe*, *Don Juan*, and *The Misanthrope* are plays whose titles have been familiar to theatergoers for hundreds of years.

Molière was heavily influenced by Italian theater, particularly the *commedia dell'arte* troupes he encountered on his tours. He tamed the rambunctiousness of those performances, refining them and coming up with his own, less frivolous style.

Molière was admired by King Louis XIV's brother, who became his patron. Later, Moliere was appointed an official provider of entertainment to the Sun King himself.

Jean Racine (1639-1699)

Not only a contemporary of Molière, Racine also had several of his early plays produced by the elder playwright.

While many other playwrights of the period chose to concentrate on comedy and satire, Racine was obsessed with tragedy; he also wrote elegant and melancholy poetry. As a playwright, Racine often wrestled with the classical theme of man's struggle with an unchangeable fate. His excruciating exploration of the passions of humanity and of his characters—particularly their motives—are the ingredients that give his work a sustaining voice. Though Racine was at first imitative of Pierre Corneille, his skill and status improved, and soon came to rival those of the earlier writer. Theatergoers today know Racine for such pieces as *Phedre*, *Britannicus*, and *Andromaque*.

Music

The idea of dualism is probably what best sums up the transition from the Renaissance to the early Baroque, not only in musical innovations but in most other aspects as well. There was an appreciation of the often startling contrasts when old ideas coexisted with new, when big stood next to small, when ornate was considered along with the ordinary. Dualism is a significant ingredient in the development of Baroque music, which built substantially on the Renaissance ideal of counterpoint, and which also saw the rise of instrumental forms that did not rely on voices (though voices remained important to Baroque composers).

Dualism may have inspired the characteristic "give and take" of Baroque musical forms—vocals

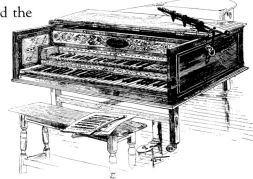

Above: A fanciful rendering of a typical informal gathering of musicians in the Baroque. Right: The harpsichord was a principal instrument in Baroque era music.

J. S. Bach's manuscript for a solo violin sonata.

opposing instrumentals, soloists opposing the orchestral group, and so on. Nevertheless, it is a cooperative opposition that heightens Baroque music's emotional impact rather than leading it into chaos. Sometimes existing as undercurrents in an otherwise smoothly flowing piece, the oppositions are sometimes manifested more clearly when one section of the orchestra takes the lead for several measures, another section answers, and the first takes up the lead again, resulting in a musical tug of war.

The Baroque was primarily a musician's era. While music in the late Renaissance had become quite complex—vocal and instrumental counterpoint were highly developed—instruments were used mostly as a platform to showcase or accentuate lyrics. In contrast, what became paramount during the Baroque was the message the music itself could convey. The intricacies of instrumental harmony were advanced through the use of *basso continuo* and tonality. Long-form music for instrumental soloists or groups, such as sonatas and concertos, was developed. Musical notation (as in *allegro, adagio, forte,* etc.) was introduced to indicate tempo and emotion. The concept of instrumental improvisation developed: Baroque composers often did not write solo parts into their pieces; instead, they made nota-tions, the equivalent of "insert solo here," and musicians were expected to improvise. Likewise, in basso continuo, harmony parts for the bass accompaniment were often noted on sheet music only as single numbers. The

The Servais Cello. a Stradivarius, is on display at the Smithsonian Institution

Instruments were handcrafted by skilled artisans, often in family workshops.

accompanist was expected to translate the number into the musical interval above or below a particular note and improvise, or "realize," the harmony. For the first time, because of these experiments in harmony and tonality, compositions often started in one key and ended in another, a Baroque innovation called modulation.

The beginning of the Baroque era also corresponds with the emergence in Italy of the vocal music that eventually became opera. In Florence, during the last decade of the 1500s, a group of intellectuals calling themselves the Camerata began reviving  Greek tragedies using a device now called monody, an emotional, expressive, solo vocal piece with sparse accompaniment that eventually came to be called an aria.

The Camerata realized that the popular Renaissance madrigal was not the right platform for the kind of storytelling it wanted to do, and a theater

Interior of the Regio Theater, Turin, Italy.

George Frideric Handel (1685-1759)

Though born in Germany, Handel spent most of his adult life in England and is buried in London's Westminster Abbey. (Remarkably, Handel's considerable talent, which manifested itself when he was very young, was discouraged by his father for many years.) As a young man, he traveled extensively, spending four years in Italy where he became adept at the Italian musical style. While there he wrote two oratorios (the form for which he is most renowned), and an opera (a form for which he is also remembered).

On his return to Germany, Handel was appointed musical director to the royal house in Hanover: this appointment would recommend him when, soon after, he moved to England.

It was during a visit to England in 1711 to see a performance of his successful opera *Rinaldo* that Handel evidently decided he would like to live there permanently. After a brief return to Germany, Handel settled in London, eventually becoming a British citizen. Three years later, in 1714, his former employer in Hanover became King George I of England, guaranteeing an agreeable start to Handel's new life as a British subject. The transplanted German became director of the Royal Academy of Music and also of the Second Academy. He was London's leading composer and director of Italian Opera and was, in fact, a leading Baroque composer of the form.

Famous also as the composer of the oratorio *Messiah*, Handel contributed brilliantly to English choral music.

Handel's original score for Messiah.

Published manuscript of Handel's opera Julius Caesar.

A fanciful cover of a biography of Monteverdi.

style was developed in which arias were linked together by recitatives—less musical vocal parts meant mostly to advance the story. The new form was quickly embraced and spread to Rome, Venice, and Naples where it was enhanced and embellished. Claudio Monteverdi (1567-1643), the undisputed master of the madrigal and a genius of both the late Renaissance and early Baroque, debuted his opera *Orfeo* in 1607. It contained arias, recitatives, and madrigal-like instrumental parts. In Rome, themes for operas shifted away from Greek myth and legend, and toward religion. In Venice the first public opera house opened in 1637. But it was

Alessandro Scarlatti.

A view of Naples.

Naples that became the center of Italian opera in the latter half of the 1600s, and from there the form spread throughout Europe.

Neapolitan opera stressed the aria. Orchestra, chorus, and recitative parts played less significant roles, and sometimes were not employed at all. Alessandro Scarlatti (1660-1725) was the premier composer of Neapolitan opera, and completed 114 during his career. George Frideric Handel (1685-1759), a German who spent many years in England, also composed operas in the Neapolitan style during the Baroque.

Johann Sebastian Bach (1685-1750)

He held a number of patronage posts throughout his later life, mostly with churches. He fathered twenty children, several of them becoming talented musicians in their own right: Johann Christian, Carl Philipp Emanuel, and Wilhelm Freidemann. It was his association with the church that required him to compose and perform sacred music. He is also known to have experimented with musical theory and structure, composing great works that were never publicly performed in his lifetime. The Mass in B Minor and *The Art of the Fugue* are two such. *The Art of the Fugue*, unfinished at his death, was an immensely intricate exploration of a form that Bach evidently knew was falling out of fashion.

Bach's death in 1750 officially brought the Baroque era to an end.

Arguably the greatest composer in Western musical history, Bach was better known in his lifetime as an organist, though his musical and keyboard innovations often got him into trouble with employers and audiences who found them too startling.

During his lifetime, Bach produced more than one thousand compositions in virtually every form and genre of his day. Many—sacred and secular, choral and instrumental—are now considered masterpieces. It is believed that his output was even more prolific, but that a great many of his works, cantatas and oratorios in particular, were lost.

Born into a family of musicians in Eisenach, Germany, Bach was orphaned at nine and went to live with his brother, who himself was an organist.

A cantata in Leipzig, 1732.

Original manuscript of J. S. Bach's Invention No. 8.

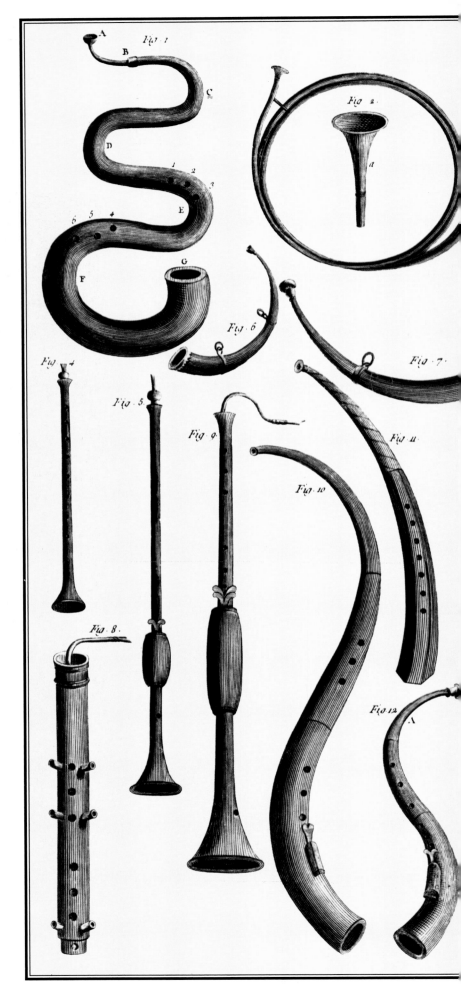

The new forms that arose during the Baroque manifested themselves differently in different places. French opera and what was called "dramatic music" in England and Germany were very different from Italian opera and from each other. As with other forms of artistic expression, Baroque music was shaped by the norms of the prevailing culture. The French, for example, put ballet into their operas and stressed drama and orchestration far more than did the Italians. Even though Handel wrote opera while living in London, the English didn't appreciate the form nearly as enthusiastically as everyone else. They did, however, put on their own version—lavish masques, which were plays mostly on mythological topics, that included songs, poetry readings, choruses, instrumentation, and occasionally, recitatives and dances. German opera was called *Singspiel*, but that form referred mostly to the later comic operas. Early German opera was based almost exactly on the Italian model, and usually the Germans watched Italian companies perform their own creations.

Religion and politics played major roles in how music was written, although it was

An assortment of Baroque woodwind instruments, including: clarino, cornetto, corna da caccia, crumhorn, curtal, hautbois, sacbut, serpent, shawm.

Antonio Vivaldi (1678-1741)

Known as "the Red Priest" because of his red hair, Vivaldi stopped saying Mass soon after his ordination in 1703 and pursued a career as a violinist, entrepreneur, and composer.

He traveled extensively, producing operas throughout Europe, many of them his own. While he is known to have boasted and perhaps even exaggerated about the number of his own compositions, at least 450 concertos by Vivaldi have recently been found.

For reasons that are still not clear, Vivaldi was forgotten almost immediately after he died, impoverished, in Vienna. The whereabouts of the bulk of his work was unknown for more than a century. But many manuscripts by the Italian virtuoso were uncovered in this century, by scholars who were researching the work of J. S. Bach. Fortunately for Vivaldi, he had made an impression on Bach, who even arranged for the keyboard some of the Italian's violin concertos.

That brush with Bach more than two hundred years ago assured that the music of the once-forsaken Vivaldi would eventually be rediscovered, recorded, and admired by an audience far larger than the one he had had while he lived.

Relatively new in the Baroque era, the double bass descended from the viol.

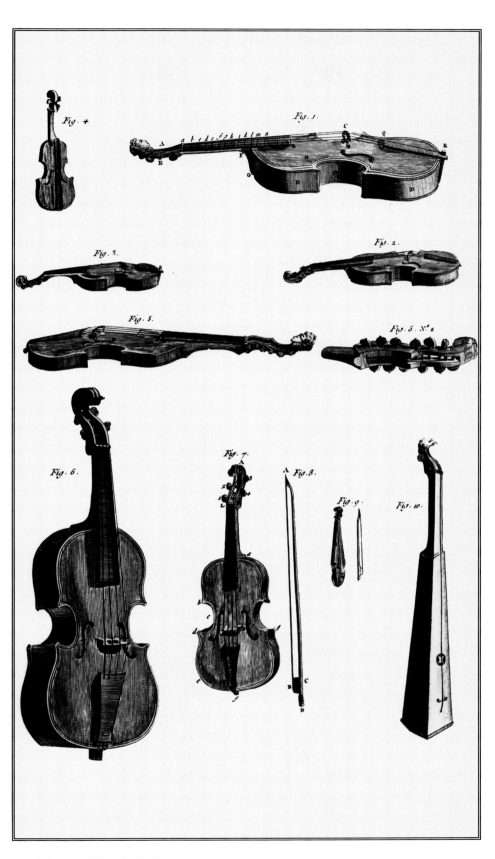

Members of the violin family.

during the Baroque that patronage from both church and state began to take a back seat to private commissions, paid admission to public concerts, and performance royalties. As colonialism enriched Europe, the emerging middle class demanded, and could pay for, musical entertainment. Once the sole domain of the church, royalty, and the wealthy, music became available to nearly everyone during the Baroque.

Still, the Church had considerable influence on many composers and exercised it during the Counter Reformation. Liturgical music, religious music written for use in church ceremonies, was a significant product of the Baroque era. Nonliturgical music, religious in nature but not intended for church ceremonies, also flourished. Catholic strongholds such as Rome and some of the imperial European cities kept alive the Renaissance a capella tradition in both forms. In other, less parochial areas, or in Protestant strongholds, masses and motets were often written in the new style, and sometimes were as lavish and flashy as operas. The reality was that composers often wrote whatever they wanted. Johann

While dance music was a fundamental Baroque form, not all of it was meant for dancing.

Sebastian Bach's Mass in B Minor, written for the Catholic service, is as grand a spectacle as anything produced during the Baroque. Bach also wrote more than two hundred cantatas, the principal form of Protestant church music.

The clavicembalo a coda—
a harpsichord.

Oratorios were another Baroque innovation. George Frideric Handel perfected this form, which is a distinct offshoot of opera and uses arias, recitative, chorus, and orchestration, but no scenery or costumes. The *Messiah* is the most famous of Handel's more than twenty oratorios.

Dance music was both fun and important for Baroque composers. A lively or pleasing dance suite could do wonders for a musician's standing with his patron. Dance music was not always meant for dancing, however—much of it was intended for listening. Dances were usually composed in sets called suites or partitas. The instrumentation was usually a harpsichord or clavichord, a chamber ensemble, and sometimes an orchestra. Some of the most popular Baroque dance types were the slow *sarabande*, the moderately fast *allemande*, the somewhat faster *courante*, and the very lively *gigue*, which usually was the last movement in a particular partita.

The Brandenburg Concertos

The six Brandenburg Concertos were written over a considerable period of time and not necessarily in the order in which they are currently numbered. They are significant because Bach introduced unusual instrumental elements into the majority of the Brandenburgs that do not appear in other contemporary concerti grossi, which featured solo parts for stringed instruments almost exclusively. They were assembled by Bach in 1721 and presented to the orchestra of Christian Ludwig, Margrave (prince) of Brandenburg, an important German nobleman whom Bach may have met two years earlier in Berlin.

At the time he presented the Brandenburgs, Bach was working in Cöthen, Germany, having moved there from Weimar, where for nine years he had been court organist. The No. 5 Concerto is thought to be the last one composed in the set, almost certainly in Cöthen. It includes Bach's first use of the transverse flute paired with violin, but it is primarily a harpsichord concerto and marks the inauguration of that form.

Bach's Brandenburg Concerto No. 5 in D Major *is a showcase for the harpsichord.*

Gaspar Netscher's Viol da Gamba Lesson *hangs in the Louvre.*

Sonatas and concertos were two great innovations of the middle Baroque and answered the main puzzle posed at the beginning of the era: how to sustain interest in a long-form musical composition in which there was no singing. Broadly speaking, sonatas were works for one or more solo instruments; concertos were compositions for orchestral groups.

There are different kinds of sonatas and concertos. The major sonata forms came about gradually during the early 1600s and, through experimentation and innovation, evolved from single, long-form solo pieces into multi-movement works. The unaccompanied solo sonata features either violin, cello, or harpsichord, the accompanied solo sonata requires at least three instruments, usually violin, cello, and harpsichord with basso continuo provided by either the cello or harpsichord; and the most important Baroque sonata form, the trio sonata, generally was performed with four instruments.

Concertos too came in different flavors. Originally, concerto was used to describe a composition for voices that also had instrumental parts, but around 1650 the word began to refer to a purely orchestral piece in

Alessandro Marcello (1684-1750)

Even though his younger brother Benedetto wrote far more music, Alessandro Marcello is a better example of Venetian *nobile dilettante*—a man for whom the composing and performing of music was an enchantment rather than a livelihood. Alessandro Marcello's musical output was sparse, but it was only one part of an active, creative imagination that also produced poetry of distinction, painting, singing, and serious work in philosophy and mathematics.

Marcello's Oboe Concerto in D Minor was regarded highly enough in his day to have attracted the attention of Johann Sebastian Bach, who embellished it slightly and transcribed it for keyboard (BMV 974). Bach may have been under the impression that he was transcribing a piece by Antonio Vivaldi, who was a contemporary of Marcello, a fellow Venetian, and the author of a multitude of compositions. There was a lot of confusion about the true authorship of the concerto, which later still was attributed to Marcello's brother Benedetto. Researchers eventually discovered a published copy of the concerto in its original key, with Alessandro named as the composer.

In his published music (twelve cantatas, a set of concertos, and a set of violin sonatas), Alessandro shows himself to have been a superb craftsman, concerned with giving a unique voice to each of his compositions. This contrasts with many of the lesser composers of his day, who often based new pieces on themes they had already explored.

which groups of instruments "opposed" each other in the characteristic Baroque style. The *concerto grosso* was the Baroque's most important orchestral form. It was written for what are called the *tutti* and *concertino* groups within an orchestral ensemble; the concertino was a small array of two or three solo instruments, usually strings, that played against the remainder of the group (tutti). The opposition was usually in alternating sections within a movement, but sometimes the contrast was written as an ongoing battle.

Of the instrumental advances made during the Baroque, the invention of the fortepiano and the development of the violin family rank at the top of the list, even though virtually no Baroque music was composed for the piano. Technological advancements brought improvements to existing instruments such as the organ, harpsichord, and woodwinds. The lute faded from popularity.

Bartolomeo Cristofori invented the fortepiano (literally, "loud-soft") in Florence in 1709, a full forty years before the "official" end of the Baroque era. Its hammer and sustain abilities were primitive by today's standards, but they allowed musicians a greater dynamic range than did the plucking action of the harpsichord. While this breakthrough for the keyboard ought to have captured the imagination of Baroque composers and performers, it apparently did not. It was not until the late 1700s that the fortepiano became widely recognized and used. The violin family, however, caught on rapidly when its various members were developed from the viol family around 1700.

The Baroque did not end abruptly. Some of its forms and fashions were summarily dropped, but many others either gradually faded away, or were transformed by later innovations into the emerging pre-Classical and Classical periods. Again, culture and geography played a major part. In France, the light and ornate Rococo style was definitely a backlash against the heavy, ponderous High Baroque. The Germans evidently liked

Nicholas Tournier's The Concert *hangs in the Louvre.*

Arcangelo Corelli (1653-1713)

An Italian violinist and composer, Corelli is noted for his contributions to the trio sonata and concerto grosso forms.

Corelli, born near Bologna, was employed most of his life in Rome by a number of the leading music patrons of his day. He was a leader of the instrumental section of Rome's prestigious Academy of Santa Cecilia and served for a time as violin virtuoso and music director for Rome's celebrated music patron, Cardinal Pietro Ottoboni.

Corelli wrote nearly fifty trio sonatas, twelve solo violin sonatas, and at least twelve concerti grossi.

Below: Manuscript for a Corelli trio sonata.

An altar in the Baroque Church of St. Ignatius, Rome.

the heavyhandedness and carried on with their *Sturm und Drang* literary period and their more elegant *Empfindsamer Stil*. But even with the emergence of new styles, there is no clear demarcation between the Baroque and what came next. As in the beginning of the Baroque era, when Monteverdi composed in both the *stile antico* (old, Renaissance style) and *stile moderno* (new style), many Baroque composers began shifting with the tide, at first mixing styles and ultimately contributing fully to the new order. Others, Like J. S. Bach, whose death in 1750 marks the end of the era, were never able to adapt, or didn't want to. Bach, the greatest musician of the Baroque, went to his grave knowing that his work was thought by many to be stodgy, pretentious, and out of date.

Glossary

A capella: Vocal music without instrumental accompaniment.

Adagio: Musical notation indicating a slow tempo. (Faster than largo but not as fast as andante.)

Allegro: Musical notation originally indicating a cheerful or joyous rendition of a musical passage. It now indicates a fast tempo. (Quicker than andante, but not as fast as presto.)

Allemande: Moderately fast dance music in double-time (2/4, for example). It probably originated in Germany; it was popular in France after 1500 and later in England.

Andante: Musical notation indicating a moderate tempo. (Faster than adagio but slower than allegro.)

Basso continuo: A bass part, often for keyboard or strings, consisting of a succession of bass notes with figures indicating the musical intervals at which an improvised accompaniment could be played. Also called figured bass or thoroughbass.

Cadenza: An (occasionally) improvised passage near the end of a solo piece that served to show off technical skill.

Cantata: The most important vocal form of the Baroque, usually consisting of two or three elaborate solo songs connected by recitatives.

Concertino: A small group of soloists within an orchestra. Usually two violins and a cello, accompanied by a harpsichord.

Concerto grosso: A multimovement instrumental piece in which a small group of soloists (concertino) alternates back and forth with the full orchestra (tutti).

Courante: Lively dance music in triple-time (usually 3/4 or 3/8).

Forte: Musical notation indicating that a passage should be played loudly.

Fugue: A simple musical statement that is repeated and interwoven by different parts of a multivoice ensemble.

Gigue: Fast and lively dance music that generally concluded a Baroque era suite. The gigue probably descended from Irish and English jigs.

Improvisation: The "invention" of music as it is being played. Usually, a soloist playing with a larger group is called upon to improvise, or "make up," a part that complements the piece of music being played.

Largo: Musical notation indicating a very slow tempo.

Madrigal: A type of poem set to music that first evolved in Italy. At first, it required two voice parts and simple accompaniment. At its peak in the sixteenth century, madrigals were written for any number of elaborate voice parts with equally elaborate counterpoint accompaniment, generally by stringed instruments.

Masque: A short dramatic piece performed by masked actors, often accompanied by music.

Mass: An important form of sacred music for voices and instruments, performed during the Catholic rite, written in two sections: the Ordinary and the Proper.

Modulation: A change of key within a composition.

Monody: Expressive, dramatic single-voice song, usually with simple accompaniment.

Motet: Originally a vocal style of sacred music. By the Baroque, motets came to include instrumental accompaniment, arias, and recitatives.

Opera buffa: Comic opera.

Opera seria: Serious or tragic opera.

Oratorio: Essentially an opera without scenery, costumes, or acting. The story, usually based on the Bible, is told by a chorus, orchestra, soloists, and sometimes a narrator.

Presto: Musical notation indicating a very fast tempo.

Recitative: Singing style with little change in pitch that imitates the natural inflections of speech.

Sarabande: Dance music in triple-time (3/4 or 3/8) that was slow, stately, and often mournful.

Sonata: A three- or four-movement piece for solo instrument, or for two instruments with one designated the lead, the other as accompaniment.

Suite: Instrumental music that, during the Baroque, was a composition in four parts, each in a different tempo. The music was usually "stylized dance" music, meaning no one actually danced to it. Generally, the four parts of a suite were the allemande (moderate), courante (fast), sarabande (slow) and gigue (fast). Also called partita.

Tutti: An indication for all parts of an ensemble to play together.

Listener's Guide

Johann Sebastian Bach (1685-1750)
The Hunting Cantata, BWV 208 (1716)
Trio Sonata No. 1 in E-flat Major,
BWV 525 (c. 1727)
Prelude and Fugue in E-flat
("St. Anne's"), BWV 552 (1739)
Toccata and Fugue in D Minor,
BWV 565 (c. 1708)
The Well-Tempered Clavier, Book I,
BWV 846-869 (1722)
The Well-Tempered Clavier, Book II,
BWV 870-893 (1738-1742)
Chromatic Fantasia and Fugue in
D Minor, BWV 903 (1738)
Aria and 30 Variations ("Goldberg
Variations"), BWV 988 (1741)
Aria and Variations in the Italian Style,
BWV 989 (pre-1714)
Brandenburg Concertos Nos. 1-6,
BWV 1046-1051 (c. 1718-1720)
Italian Concerto in F, BWV 971 (1735)
Suites for Unaccompanied Cello Nos. 1-6,
BWV 1007-1012 (c. 1720)
Sonatas for Viola da Gamba and
Harpsichord Nos. 1-3,
BWV 1027-1029 (1720)
The Art of the Fugue, BWV 1080 (1749)

Francesco Cavalli (1602-1676)
Operas:
Egisto (1643)
Giasone (1648)
Calisto (1651)
Xerse (1654)

Arcangelo Corelli (1653-1713)
Trio Sonatas Nos. 1-12, Op. 1 (1681)
Violin Sonatas Nos. 1-12, Op. 5 (1700)
Concerti Grossi Nos. 1-12, Op. 6 (1714)

Girolamo Frescobaldi (1583-1643)
Partite sopra l'aria della Romanesca (1616)
Correnti Nos. 1-4 (1616)
Toccata Prima (1627)
Capriccio sopra la bassa fiammenga (1624)
Capriccio di durezze (1624)
Galiards Nos. 1-5 (1627)
35 Canzoni (1628)

George Frideric Handel (1685-1759)
Suites in F Major, G Major, D Major
("Water Music," 1715-1717)
Six Fugues or Voluntarys for Organ
or Harpsichord (1735)
Concerti Grossi Op. 3 (1734)
Concerti for Harpsichord or Organ,
Op. 4 (1738)
Concerti Grossi Nos. 1-12,
("Grand Concertos"), Op. 6 (1739)
Oratorios:
Rinaldo (1711)
Ode for St. Cecilia's Day (1738)
Israel in Egypt (1739)
Messiah (1741)
Samson (1743)

Benedetto Marcello (1686-1739)
Canzoni madrigalesche per camera (1717)
Il pianto e il riso delle quattro stagioni
dell'anno (1731)
Il trionfo della Poesia e della Musica (1733)

Claudio Monteverdi (1567-1643)
Madrigals Books 1-6 (1587-1614)
Scherzi Musicali a tre voci (1607)
Operas:
L'Orfeo (1607)
L'Arianna (1608)

Henry Purcell (1659-1695)
Opera:
Dido & Aneas (1689)
Overture to Timon of Athens (1694)
Hail Bright Cecilia (1692)
Suites:
The Gordian Knot Untied (1691)
The Virtuous Wife (c. 1694)

Alessandro Scarlatti (1660-1725)
Operas:
Gli equivoci nel sembiante (1679)
Il Mitridate Eupatore (1707)
Il tigrane (1715)
Serenatta: Diana & Endimione (1679-85)
Cantatas:
Solitudini amene, bersaglio (1705)
Andante, o miei sospiri ("Con idea
inhumama") (1712)
Oratorios:
L'assunzione della Beata Vergine
Maria (1703)
San Filippo Neri (1705)
Oratorio per la Santissima Annunziata
(1708)
Variations on "La follia" (1715)
St. John Passion (c. 1680)
St. Cecilia Mass (1720)
12 Sinfonie di concerto grosso
(begun 1715)

Domenico Scarlatti (1685-1757)
30 sonatas for Harpsichord (1738)

Georg Philipp Telemann (1681-1767)
Concerto in F-sharp Minor for Violin
Concerto in E Minor for Oboe, Strings,
and Continuo
Concerto in D Major for 3 Trumpets,
2 Oboes, Tympani, Strings, and
Continuo
Cantata cycle: Der Harmonische
Gottes-Dienst (1725-1726)
Suite in E Minor ("Table Music"),
Part I (1733)

Antonio Vivaldi (1678-1741)
12 Concerti, Op. 3 (L'estro Armonico)
12 Concerti, Op. 4 (La Stravaganza)
12 Concerti, Op. 8 (Il cimento dell'armonia
e dell'invenzione; includes Four Seasons)
12 Violin Concerti, Op. 9
(La Cetra, 1727)

Reader's Guide

•• Borroff, Edith. *Music of the Baroque.* Dubuque, Iowa: W.C. Brown Co., 1970.

•• Palisca, Claude V. *Norton Anthology of Western Music,* Vol. I. New York: Norton, 1980.

•• Palisca, Claude V. *Prentice Hall History of Music Series: Baroque Music,* 3rd ed. Englewood Cliffs, NJ: 1991.

•• Rosenstiel, gen. ed. *Schirmer History of Music.* New York: Schirmer, 1982.

•• Sadie, Julie Anne, ed. *Companion to Baroque Music.* London: J.M. Dent and Sons, 1990.

•• Sadie, Stanley, ed. *Grove's Dictionary of Music.* London: Macmillan, 1980.

Photography & Illustration Credits

Index